Fame Whore

Tom Ratcliffe

with lyrics by Gigi Zahir

T0021636

methuen | drama

LONDON • NEW YORK • OXFORD • NEW DELHI • SYDNEY

METHUEN DRAMA
Bloomsbury Publishing Plc
50 Bedford Square, London, WC1B 3DP, UK
1385 Broadway, New York, NY 10018, USA
29 Earlsfort Terrace, Dublin 2, Ireland

BLOOMSBURY, METHUEN DRAMA and the Methuen
Drama logo are trademarks of Bloomsbury Publishing Plc

First published in Great Britain 2022

First published in Great Britain 2022

A catalogue record for this book is available from the British Library.

A catalog record for this book is available from the Library of Congress.

ISBN: PB: 978-1-3503-7835-3
ePDF: 978-1-3503-7837-7
eBook: 978-1-3503-7836-0

Series: Modern Plays

Typeset by Mark Heslington Ltd, Scarborough, North Yorkshire

To find out more about our authors and books visit
www.bloomsbury.com and sign up for our newsletters.

Special thanks to Matthew Baldwin, Vanessa Passing and Thursday

First performed at the King's Head Theatre, October 2022

Full team – King's Head October 2022

Becky Biro   **Gigi Zahir**

Writer/Director	Tom Ratcliffe
Lyrics	Gigi Zahir
Producer	Sarah Allen
Assistant Director	Sophia Utria
Assistant Producer	Harris Albar
Set Designer	Alys Whitehead
Lighting Designer	Hugo Dodsworth
Sound Designer	Jac Cooper
Costume Designer	Miss Jake
Videographer	Jayd Kent
Projection Realisation	Frances Ashton
Backing Tracks	Mark Fenton
Stage Manager	Naomi Denny
Assistant Stage Manager	Bethany Gemmell

Tom Ratcliffe

Tom is an award-winning, internationally produced writer /
actor and is Co Executive Director of Wildcard. Recent
commisions include writing for Harlow Playhouse. Tom's
play *Evelyn* ran at the Southwark Playhouse and Mercury
Theatre starring Rula Lenska. Writing credits include:
Wreckage (Summerhall); *Evelyn* (Southwark Playhouse /
Mercury Theatre); *Velvet* (UK and Ireland tour / Pleasance
Courtyard); *Circa* (Theater de Meervaart, Amsterdam / The
Old Red Lion) and *Gifted* (Pleasance Theatre). Tom was
awarded the J.B. Priestley Award for Writers of Promise in
2020. He was shortlisted for the Old Vic 12 in 2016 and has
been longlisted for the Verity Bargate, Theatre503 and
Papatango playwriting awards. Short plays have included
runs at Theatre503, Old Red Lion Theatre and the St
James's Theatre.

Gigi Zahir

Gigi Zahir is an American-born, London-based actor, singer,
comedian, writer, producer and emcee, though they are more
widely known as their drag alter ego Crayola The Queen.
After graduating from the Stella Adler Studio of Acting in
2016 and interning at the Cincinnati Playhouse in the Park in
2017, Gigi made the decision to step away from theatre to
focus on queer cabaret and solo performance. The last year
has seen them return to the theatre world with their drag
skills in tow, recently putting a very queer spin on Trinculo in
Wildcard's *Tempest* at The Pleasance, which *The Independent*
called 'riotously funny' and What's On Stage said 'they have
the audience eating out of the palm of their hand'. Gigi hopes
to continue weaving back and forth between theatre, drag
and cabaret in the future, and cherishes any chance to see
these different modes intertwine. You can find out more
about them at www.CrayolaTheQueen.com, and if you'd like
to connect on socials it's @CrayolaTheQueen on all
platforms.

Sarah Allen

Sarah Allen is a producer from Somerset currently based in London. Her work frequently focuses on expanding the practice of producing with an emphasis on wellbeing, collaboration, and transparency. She also regularly works as an access support worker for artists working in theatre. In 2020 she graduated from the Royal Central School of Speech and Drama with an MA in Creative Producing and has recently worked on projects at Soho Theatre, Theatre503, Battersea Arts Centre and the Royal Vauxhall Tavern.

Fame Whore

Characters

Becky Biro
Producer
Cindy Sawfoot
David Peckham
Presenter 1
Presenter 2
Reporter 1
Reporter 2
Madonna
Interviewer
Jackie Beaver
Voica Reesin
Julie's iPad
Albert Brewerton
Aveek Tim

All characters in the originating production were played by the same actor. All characters other than **Becky Biro** *were realised either through video design or voice over.*

Notes on Text

Becky Biro *is the central character to be taken on by the actor. Other characters can be recorded voices or played by the actor.*

Pauses and beats are indicated by the space given between lines.

/ Indicates that the next line should start and overlap.

– Indicates an interruption by the following line.

One

Becky Biro is a good person and all of this just happened upon her

Becky   Ummm

Being community minded?
Like
When I feel there's
Umm
Injustice or inequality happening I
Like
Activate mama bear mode
Like
Hey
Fuck you homophobe
I'm about to rip your cunt face off and feed it to Goldilocks
Ha
No but seriously I go into super protective mode because it's
just so important to me
It's why Madonna
All praise the holy mother of pop
Is one of my biggest inspirations
She was standing up for our rights and shit
You know
Being an ally at a time when not many people were
This stuff matters
I can get pretty angry and mouthy about it
I probably get quite scary sometimes

Producer   Scary?
Interesting

Becky   Well that's not
I feel like maybe I got myself into a
Word vomit wormhole there because Becky Biro's best
quality is bringing the colour and the joy to this increasingly
dark and depressing world
You know

Drag is
I see drag as an active service to the community
It's not just about love and adoration for doing a 'death drop'
You have to do the work
It's my job to make people's worlds a little brighter
Educated and enlightened
So Becky is like
Delicious and good tasting but also nutritious having some vitamins and minerals all up in there too
It's not just donuts for dinner

She notices the **Producer** *furiously taking notes.*

Becky   I've got like a big
Um
World is flat mentality
Not like a flat earther
God no
That would just be
Imagine
Becky Trump
But I mean world is flat in the sense that like
There is no hierarchy

Producer   Are you a fan of the show Becky?

Becky   Sorry?

Producer   Do you like the show?

Becky   Absolutely
Are you kidding?
I'm a crazy big fan
Superfan
Fan girly fan fan
All the fans
Fan

Producer   Really?

Becky   Absolutely yeah
Duh

Producer   You've been quite critical
Overtly critical actually
Publicly
Online
Which just makes us question why you should come on the
show?
Why you would want to come on the show?

Becky   I
I thought you might ask me this
And I think that
As with any fan of any TV show
It's easy to get caught up in the moment
In the discourse and
Contribute to that
Online
In the form of a hot take
Or several hot takes
As the case may be

It's not that I don't stand by some of what I said I just think
that
Unlike some of the other contestants
I would be able to use my platform for good
To set an example
If that makes sense?

Producer   Look
Becky
We've been here before
Several years in a row now and I'm just gonna be real with you

Becky   Okay

Producer   You've threatened the show
You and several others
You've threatened our reputation and standing within the
community with what you've been saying

Becky   I would hardly say –

Producer   So
Let's face it
It's probably not gonna happen unless you can bring
something to the show
Offer something for us
And right now you're an unknown quantity
So

Becky   So I need to increase my following?

Producer   It's not just
Um
You would need a profile
Yeah
Enough to convince the bigger bosses
The powers that be
To bring you on

Becky   Right

I get that

Becky Biro *is streaming live on social media.*

Becky   Cindy Sawfoot isn't just my drag sister
She's my soul sister
And I know what y'all are thinking
That it must be difficult for me having a best friend who's so
Yeah
I guess she is my best friend
Sorry
Sidetrack
If you're new to me you'll soon pick up that I do this a lot
I'll be doing a show
Or a live
And I'll be on talking trash singing about one thing or
another

Then suddenly I'm like
Oooh
Piece of candy
And before I know it it's 4 a.m. and I'm still streaming live to
one poor person
Lipsyncing the theme tune of what's the story of Balamory
that nobody wants know

Oh hey Warmie69
That's cute. Thanks for stopping by
I can see y'alls comments I'll get back to those in a sec

Right Becky
Shake it out
Focus
What I'm saying is, you messy kittens out there must think
that having a best friend
Like Cindy
You know
The one from the telly who's suddenly been platformed in
such a humongous
Megatronic
Is that is word?
Way
Must be really difficult for me
And that I must be filled to the brim with envy
Well
Let me tell you now my little snugglepuffs
In the sacred
Beholden and immortal words of he who is Skepta
That's not me

And I'm not saying this in like a boastful
I'm holier than thou way
Of course I get jealous
We've all felt the lurking of the green eyed monster hiding
underneath our skinbeds
I mean hell
We drag amphibians get ass fucked with no lube by said

monster all the time
But when it comes to my drag family
My friends
I just get so overwhelmed with a tidal wave of pride that I
could punch myself in the face with a cheese grater and still
cry happy tears
I'm so proud of her
Her talent
And the way she uses her platform
Life's too short to be spreading anything other than positive
energy into this world

That said
All future performances from our little duo
The Powderpuff Swirls
Will just be featuring me
Cindy is very
VERY busy and we cannot guarantee her availability
For the avoidance of doubt all gigs that will not feature
Cindy will be performed under
The Powderpuff Swirl
Singular

Now I've seen lots of the Drag Factor fandom vocalising that
this might be because I've been
A little vocal
About the show since my sissy's season
So let me set this record straight
My criticism of the show and how some of the girls use their
platforms has nothing to do with Cindy's success and how
Cindy uses her platform
I love the show I just wish that it was more inclusive and
used it's platforms to celebrate all drag as opposed to one
subsection of our community
Our sabbatical is merely because Cindy has other
commitments right now which obviously take precedence
I am not bitter and jealous of her success and that doesn't
even make sense
We are all on our own path and one person's success does

not detract from anyone else's
And also
What is success?
Huge platform and notoriety isn't necessarily everyone's
barometer of achievement

Oh hey I can see we have some new faces logging on
If you like colourful things
Rainbows happiness sunshine butterflies and unicorns
Puppies and kittens and ben and jerry's phish food then feel
free to follow to get your fill of this nourishing wholesome
content

In fact you can do that now
If you click my face in the corner
Yep
That's it
Then the blue follow button
Yep
Tap it
You're done
Welcome hunny

So
In short
Y'all Biro haters out there can pipe down with that negative
energy your pumping into my space and stop jumping to
conclusions about what I want from my career
Because it's not necessarily that

Will You Follow Me

Hey Warmie69
It's been so lovely chatting
All your comments are hilarious

LMAO I'm really laughing

Yes it's true
And I hope to see way more of you Oh yes I do

Hey Miss underscore morphic
I'm so glad you dig my content
You've Liked everything on my page Feels like we've really bonded
It's so nice
Knowing you feast on me with your eyes I've got butterflies

But oh, you don't follow me Oh you don't follow me
Oh will you follow me?
Oh will you follow me? Will you follow me?

Hey Pork dot sword man
Thank you so much for your DMs Your dick pics are so beautiful Artistic, love to see them
I want more
Follow me and I'll adore
Your every pore

Hey Gothy kendolljenner
That's so cool you have a blue tick I know one day I'll have my own So tell me, how'd you get it Pretty please
Oh come on don't be a tease
Left me on read
Oh, will you follow me? Oh, will you follow me? Oh, will you follow me? Oh, will you follow me?

A hundred K seems pretty far
But I am already a star
I know one day the world will know my name And no I won't remember yours
Because I'll be famous of course
And so I'll just call everybody babe
And Pen-pals, I can promise you
I cherish every one of you
And not just cuz I need you for the fame Which I will gain

Hey pizzaslutstar
I am so close to a milestone
If only you would follow me,
I'd finally hit five thousand

Ain't that cool
Queens need a crown for them to rule And you'll be my five
thousandth jewel So pizzaslutstar here's to you
This ones for you

Oh, will you follow me? Oh, will you follow me? Oh, will you
follow me? Oh, will you follow me? Will you follow me?

And like
And comment
Because engagement
Is really fucking important
And the algorithm keeps changing
So yeah also bookmark my posts
And send them to your friends
And turn notifications on for my page
Pretty please

Cindy   We need to talk

Becky   When you first hear Cindy's voice on TV you
probably think
Wow
She's not the sharpest knife in the drawer
But Cindy's a mastermind when it comes to branding
The UK's version of Paris Hilton
And what she doesn't want you to know is that she's not from
the east end of London
She's actually from Surrey
But the minute Cindy gets drunk or the slightest bit
emotional
You hear her voice for what it truly is
Home counties realness

Cindy   I can't believe you would do this
You're a snake
You're a fucking

Becky Ever since she got famous she's been super paranoid
Like every time there's a rumour
Or some secret spread about her online
We all get an earful
No one in her life is spared
It's as if she thinks none of us actually like her and our sole purpose on this earth is to spread a nasty Twitter rumour that she gives bad blowjobs

Cindy You leaked it
On Reddit

Becky See

Cindy I know you did
Just say

Becky I personally find that the best way to deal with Cindy's outbursts is to pretend it's not actually happening

Are you joking?

Cindy No

Becky You're joking
Oh my god you bitch

Cindy I know it was you

Becky I'm not buying it hunny
Leaked what?

Cindy A picture

Becky What picture?
Your dick?
I don't have your dick pics

She has a tiny dick
She doesn't even have to tuck

Cindy My first time in drag
Student party

Us at uni
The fancy dress it wasn't even real drag I just
It was fancy dress you remember the t-shirt
I wore a t-shirt and it
It wasn't even a slur back then it wasn't seen as like a bad word
It wasn't a slur

Becky   Cindy has a history of being problematic
I love her don't get me wrong but she used to be like really insecure about ignorant-ass people confusing drag with being trans
And putting that on her
There were a couple of times when she was aggressively dismissive of trans performers
At one point before she got famous she was reported to the UK Drag Council
But before they could speak to her about it she was thrust onto Drag Factor
Reversed her image and tactically championed trans-inclusion on a large platform
They didn't follow it up 'cause she was suddenly doing 'good' on a wider scale
And she's marketable
Now she's essentially their talking head on a stick

Cindy   There was only one picture
Which you took

Becky   Is that it?

Cindy   It's a big deal

Becky   That's your evidence?

Cindy   Yeah

Becky   Did you delete it from your tagged photos?

Cindy   That's from like
The naughties
No one looks that far back sis

Becky   So you didn't delete it?

Cindy   No

Becky   So it couldn't possibly be one of the hundreds of thousands of Cindy stans who have public access to your tagged photos but instead it's definitely your best friend? Because she took the photo over a decade ago?
On a disposable camera
I just wanna be sure I've got this right

Cindy   I have responsibilities you know
Brands sponsor me I'm the face of companies worth
Billions
I am important Becky
I am an important person now
I have fans
You know
Fans relying on me

Becky   I know –

Cindy   You have no idea what that's like
What that pressure to be perfect is like

Becky   I didn't leak it
I promise

Cindy   You're sad Becky
Bitter and sad

Becky   She doesn't mean that

Cindy   Don't you dare fucking speak to me ever again

Cindy *hangs up.*

Becky   She's a nice person really
She's got a lot on she
She's under a lot of pressure
Trust me by tomorrow she'll forget that ever happened

It's sad
Not everyone's cut out for that life you know

Do you ever get those moments where you just stop and think
Wow
I'm a really good person?

Like not in a prophet sense 'cause I don't necessarily believe in religion per se
But just in terms of my characteristics
Actions
And what I project to the world
I definitely think I'm a really good person
I know I am
I actively choose to do good things
Like talk online about social issues because I actively aim to be a good person
Like if someone else who did believe in prophets called me a prophet
Just put that label on me
Prophet
Becky Biro the prophet
I'd understand
Not saying I would believe it obviously
Duh
I'm not a narcissist
But I'd get it
Yeah I think so yeah

My friend?
Sorta friend
Sorta friend friend Kris
An amazing drag king
Their king name's David Peckham
Well
He and I have a really complex relationship
And by complex I mean that he's caring
And kind
And likes me
And we've been fucking for years and I don't really know how to process that

We met gate-crashing Drag Factor-con
Cool right?
A load of under-represented drag artists got together and
literally stormed the pink carpet in an expertly
choreographed formation
We had kings
Trans dude kings like Kris
Lesbian queens, trans queens
You name it
It was beautiful and we just
Hit it off
After that we were always at the same gigs
We'd hook-up and cuddle but we were busy
I could keep it at a distance
Which is my preference when it comes to any kind of intimacy

But last year Kris got fucked up
Like really fucked
A guy followed them home when he was in full King mode
Took a rock and just
Went to town
It was

Fucking transphobes

And ever since the
Incident
I've been helping him a lot
Like a lot a lot
I was there when he was in hospital
I held his hand
Stroked his hair
I even helped him learn to walk again
I know
Very Florence Nightingale
But it's got to the point where there isn't that distance
anymore and I struggle to know how to cope with that
Recently I've been staying round their house when they're
scared or whatever

They have a thing about Friday nights
Tonight he called me as I was about to leave for a gig
I was literally out the door
He lives on a main road and there's this pub on the corner
It plays sports
And I think it was probably hearing cis men congregating
outside
You know
Lads lads lads
Drunk on their doorstep
It's triggering
I always joke that if I was to get onto Drag Factor I'd be his
queen in shining stilettos
That I'd bust the door down and whisk him away to a quiet
cottage in the middle of nowhere
No lads

So here I am again
Sacrificing my own stuff my own time
Being a good person
You know
A good friend
More than friend
Ish
Maybe
And actually I'm just
I'm really proud of me

David   Who are you talking to?

Becky   Sorry?

David   Who're you texting?
You've been on your phone all night

Becky   No one

David   Can I show you something
It's a
Just check it

Becky   He hands me his phone
He looks embarrassed
Is this his way of asking me to be his person?
He's definitely gonna ask me to be his person

David   I haven't said anything
Since
I know people won't read it but
I dunno

Becky   He's not asking
I didn't want that
I never said I wanted that

David   Can you read it?
Please?

Becky   'A little note from me . . .'
It's one of those things that people post online
Like a screenshot of notes so they can write 'til their hearts'
content

Baby it's not a note it's an essay

David   I know people won't see it

Becky   He's not wrong
He has less than a thousand followers

David   I just feel like it's something I have to do
For me
To
You know

Becky   It's about the incident
Hashtag trauma porn
Always popular

But I'm reading it and it's
It's beautiful
And heartfelt
Honest
All the reasons I mildly like the guy

But it's like an overshare you know?
And no one's gonna read it

David   Is it too much?
Becky?
Fuck it
I'm not doing it
Ignore me
Give it
Give it back

Becky   His face he's
He's so cute when he's worried about something
He's like a cartoon with his
Big eyes
His cheeks
Blushing in perfect pink circles

No it's cute
Sorry I was just
It's emotional
Post it

I hate myself

David   Are you sure?

Becky   Absolutely not
It's gonna get two likes
That's even worse than one

Do it
I'm so proud of you

Becky Biro *is streaming live on social media.*

Becky   This is 'She's so Lovely'
But I've changed it to
'Cheese is Lovely'

Cheese is Lovely

I love cheese if it's hot or cold
I love cheese when it's full of mold
I love cheese any time of day
I love every type of way

A comment appears on the live feed, it reads: 'you're a man'.

Becky *notices but carries on.*

Cheese is lovely
Cheese is lovely
Cheese is lovely
Cheese is lovely

More comments appear: 'You are brainwashing kids. Men are men, women are women. You are a confused man.'

'Men dressing like this openly now without shame. That's it. World has gone.'

Cheese is lovely
Cheese is lovely
Cheese is lovely

More comments appear: 'Snowflake faggot.'
'Women don't look like that love. Face caked in make-up. I could see that Adam's apple from the moon.'

Cheese is addicting
I can eat a whole block in one sitting
I'm not religious
But I'll gladly bow down and praise Cheesus

(*Not singing.*) Sorry everyone
It's getting a little hateful up in here this morning.

Throughout the next verse there is an onslaught of homophobic / transphobic comments.

I love them all hard to compare
I love brie swiss and camembert

The thought of cheese just makes me drool
Heaven is swimming in a fondue pool

Cheese is lovely
Cheese is /lovely –

Becky's *phone rings. We can see* **David Peckham** *is calling.*

Becky *answers.*

David   Becky you need to log off now
Something's happening

Becky   What do you mean?

David?

David   I'm coming over

Becky   What's going on?

David   Log off
Now

A jingle and short opening for breakfast show 'Morning UK' plays.
Becky *is streaming live to them.*

Presenter 1   Welcome back to Morning UK
I'm Presenter number one

Presenter 2   And I'm Presenter number two
Because misogyny is real

Presenter 1   London based drag artist Becky Biro joins us
now for their first interview since the infamous hijacking of
their social media live which saw them publicly receive vile
homophobic, transphobic and racist abuse whilst performing
Becky
Firstly
How are you doing now?

Becky   I'm pissed off

Presenter 2   Just a reminder that we are live

Becky   Sorry

Presenter 1   What is it that makes you so
Angry?

Becky   The attackers
Obviously
But it's also
The attacks
That we're here
Again
On social media
Where our safe online spaces are continually allowed to be
invaded by
Hate
And these big tech companies continue to turn a blind eye
You know this keeps happening not just to LGBTQ+ people
of course
But also people of colour
People are getting bombarded with hate aiming at all
intersections of their identities
It pisses me off

Presenter 2   I do understand that you're angry and upset
about the situation
But we do have to ask you to avoid using inappropriate
language

Becky   Oopsie

Presenter 2   We are a breakfast show and there are mums
and kids watching

Becky   Do as I do children not as I say

Presenter 1   I think the reason why the live has got so
much attention is that there was that moment
Whilst this torrent of abuse was flooding in
And your friend called you and told you to log off
You put that phone down

And it was clear that you thought
You know
Screw this

Becky   Watch that language sweetie

Presenter 1   I'm not gonna let this stop me
And you carried on the rest of the song

Becky   Cheese is lovely

Presenter 1   Yes
And I think people really resonated with that

Presenter 2   What was behind that decision to carry on despite the
Vile things people were saying?
Did you know that it would have such a big reaction?
That it would go so viral?

Becky   Of course I didn't
It wasn't calculated there wasn't the time to be that smart about it
It was a case of
I have people
A relatively small number of fans

Presenter 1   Not anymore

Becky   Well yes
There are certainly a lot more Pen-pals on hashtag TeamBiro
But the decision to carry on was that I am here in my own house
Literally and figuratively
And I'm not gonna let these
Haters
Stop me from entertaining my sweet little Pen-pals

Presenter 2   There are some out there who doubt the validity of the attack

Probably because of the decision to carry on
They say it seemed more like a PR stunt

Becky   That's ridiculous
You can see them can you not?
Y'all can all see the comments

Presenter 2   Oh I don't disagree

Becky   What could I possibly have to gain?
Do you think it's nice receiving comments like that?
Denying my identity as a non-binary person
The outright racism
People think I would do that?
That's crazy
I think people deny the validity of it all because they want to
avoid having the difficult conversations that we should be
having when incidents like this happen

Presenter 1   And what about Becky Biro?
What's next for her?
A lot of rumours about a certain very popular reality TV
show

Becky   Oh
Well
I don't know about that

Presenter 2   There's a lot of fans calling for you to be on it

Becky   Well that's very sweet and it's
You know
Nice to be appreciated like that
But for me it's much more important to be a positive role
model to my community
Anything else is just a bonus

We see a series of tweets from **Becky**, *commenting on social justice
issues. The tweets are all viral. They swell and the number of tweets*

overwhelm the stage. We see **Becky**'s *follower count. She now has over 100,000 followers.*

Producer   So I've spoken to the big bosses

Becky   Okay

Producer   It's safe to say you've been noticed

Becky   Yes?

Producer   Well
If you want it
You've got a spot on the show

Becky   Fuck you
You're kidding

Producer   Nope

Becky   Fuckoff
This is crazy

Producer   Congratulations

Becky   I'M GONNA BE ON DRAG FACTOR

The premiere for the season's launch of Drag Factor. **Becky** *is on the pink carpet.*

Reporter 1   Becky
Becky
If you could describe what we're to expect this season in
three words
What would you say?

Becky   Um
I'd say expect
Twists
Shenanigans

Aaaaand
Sisterhood

Reporter 2   Becky
You've finally followed in your sister Cindy's footsteps
What's the status of your relationship?
Can we expect you to perform together any time soon?

Becky   We're the best friends who both just happened to be
booked and busy
I'm sure we'll
You know
The Powderpuff Swirls will team up again in the future

Reporter 2   Is that a yes?

Reporter 3   Becky
Who are you wearing?

Becky   Your dad

Reporter 2   Becky
Is that a yes?

Reporter 1   Becky what does it mean to you to be part of
the show?

Becky   It means the world
I recognise the huge responsibility that being on a show like
this comes with
And I just hope that I'm able to spread a little bit of love and
joy into people's lives

Reporter 2   Becky?

Reporter 3   Becky is there anyone you'd like to send a
special mention to?

Becky   This is for
Well
You know who you are
I'm your queen in shining stilettos

Reporter 2   Becky?

Becky   I thought I answered your question

Reporter 2   It's just that
You say you're the best of friends but
In the last half an hour Cindy's gone live with some pretty
Serious
Accusations against you

Becky   What?
I don't think –

Reporter 2   She says that you engineered the hijacking of
your live
That you did it to gain enough profile get on the show

Becky   That's ridiculous
She hasn't said that
Why
Why would I do that?
That doesn't make sense

Reporter 2   She says she has proof
And she's going live with it
Any time now
Within the hour

Becky

Reporter 2   Is this true?

Becky

Reporter 2   Becky?

Becky

Reporter 2   Becky?

Becky

All Along

Who's been doing the bullying?
It's been Becky all along
Give her an Oscar so convincing
It's been Becky all along

She's insidious (ha-ha!)
So perfidious
That you haven't even noticed
And the pity is (the pity is)
Pity, pity, pity, pity

Take a look at her following
A hundred K going strong
Thanks to Becky (ha!)
Naughty Becky
It's been Becky all along!
(*To an audience member.*) And I fucked your dad too!

Two

Becky Biro is an evil bitch and this is what she really did

The audio of an old TV interview with a young Madonna in 1984 plays. **Becky** *lipsyncs Madonna's responses.*

Interviewer   Oh goodness I

Let us have a

The crowd screams.

She gets the general idea let us have
Just a couple of words alright

Err

When you went back to New York you sang with a trillion
bands
You quit and you went out on your own
Were you the least bit scared to do that?

Madonna   Not really
I think I've always had a lot of confidence in myself

Interviewer   We are
We are a couple of weeks into the new year
What do you hope will happen
Not only in 1984 but for the rest of your professional life
What are your dreams?
What's life?

Madonna   Mmmm
To rule the world

Becky   Some people say that when they're in drag they're
in armour
Battle armour
That when they're in this get up it gives them a a
Confidence
Like a supreme amount of confidence with a razor sharp
fucking edge that they can step out onto that stage
In the club
And if some drunk entitled muscle daddy
Or a reckless trashed hen
Heckles from the crowd or grabs their ass
They are equipped ready for battle to take that cunt down in
one fell swoop of a roasting
In one super fucking efficient line
And in some respects I find this to be true but not always it's
like yin or yang like I'll be super fucking confident but it can
just take the
The tiniest thing
The tiniest little thing and suddenly I'm having this outta
body experience and I'm just staring at myself
From up above
Like I'm up above just staring at myself going through the
motions on stage and I'm up there in the damp ceiling
corner of a dive bar screaming to my stupid fuck self the
deepest darkest truth
That I'm not funny
That I'm not clever

That I'm not as good as I think I am
That I'm wasting my life earning next to nothing asking
kind older men to fund me for my art wondering if perhaps
they want anything else from me for doing so or if I'm just
being conceited for even thinking that
That I'm performing in drag that everyone thinks is average
because I can't afford my rent let alone better clothes
TV has set unrealistic expectations for us regular folk
performing on the scene and maybe everyone who knows
nothing about drag is right
Maybe I'm not good enough
Maybe I'm not gonna make it

Cindy   Babe what is it?
I'm not being funny but I said don't just blanketly ring me
No cold calls
Text me
And if I'm free I'll say sure babes go on give us a ring

Becky   Sorry

Cindy   Well what is it then?
This is literally my one night off this month

Becky   I had my d –

Cindy   Actually
I'm such an idiot
I'm so glad you called

Becky   Oh
It's just that I had my –

Cindy   This is going to come as quite a shock

Becky   Okay

Cindy   Are you ready?

Becky   I'm ready

Cindy   You said that with some determination

Becky   I'm ready

Cindy   Whenever you're ready

Becky   I said I'm –

Cindy   Well
Becky Biro
You just happen to be speaking to the new face of Rio

Becky   De Janeiro?

Cindy   No silly
The drink

I know right
Massive

Becky   I didn't think they were still
Don't get me wrong
I love Rio
That sweet tropical goodness
Justice for Rio
But I didn't realise Rio was still

Cindy   It's still a thing
Gonna air online
TV
Cinemas
You name it

Becky   You got a commercial?

Cindy   Yeah
Thirty-five grand hun
I'm gonna be the face of Rio

Becky   You're doing an ad no?
An advert doesn't necessarily make you the face of –

Cindy   It's amaze I know
But my schedule is piling up and I'm shite at delivering bad
news you know I am I'm a right bat

Becky   What?

Cindy   I can't do pride
With you

Becky   But we're a duo

Cindy   I know
But my manager said I can't turn the solo gigs down
I've gotta ride the wave babes
Take the fifteen minutes while I can
It's a fickle world out there

Becky   It's a twenty-minute set it doesn't stop
It doesn't stop you doing anything you want to solo

Cindy   Everything is so busy not just pride
I love you I do but I just
It's too much it's too busy I'm so stressed you've no idea
Honestly
I just
I just need a break
From the Powderpuff Swirls

Are you okay?

Becky   I –

Cindy   I'll give you a shoutout on Twitter whenever you
perform
A retweet or whatever just let me know when you need

Becky   I didn't get it

Cindy   What do you mean?
I thought I was quite clear

Becky   I had my
My Drag Factor panel today I
I didn't get it

Cindy

Becky   I
I just called to tell you that

Cindy

Becky Just
Feeling a bit
You know
Shitty

Cindy Well what do you expect babe?
I'm not being funny

You literally dragged their arse
Hard
I told you
Do that and you won't get on

Becky I was supporting –

Cindy It's all very noble babes and I know your mate
David –

Becky He's not just my –

Cindy Whatever
I'm sure he appreciates it but you ain't the opposition leader
hun
It's not on you to solve world bloody poverty
Inequality
Climate change
Whatever
It's hard enough out here tucking yourself every night
without sabotaging the one chance you had to make a decent
coin for it

Like I've thought about this a lot actually
Like why
Why is she sticking her neck out being a saint and cutting
her face off to spite her ear?
And I thought about it babe and like
I think you're scared

Becky Scared?

Cindy   Like
I see you
And your skills and you're mega talented but I think you
think you wouldn't do well
Or you'd slip up say the wrong thing and come across as a
villain or
That you'd just fuck it up
So I think you're eliminating the chance of failure before
you can even give it a go
It's sad

Becky   I'm not
It's really not –

Cindy   I love you babe
But I'm really sorry
Gotta dash
I'm sorry about DF I really am but
Yeah
I've said it

Becky   Yeah

Cindy   Love you

Cindy *hangs up.*

Becky   She didn't mean that
She just
She says things to wind me up

Scared?
Scared that I wouldn't do well
I would kill it
I would fucking
I would fucking kill it

She's
She's so
She's so funny

Cindy Sawfoot is a Fucking Cunt

Cindy
Cindy
Cindy
Cindy
Cindy
Cindy
Cindy
Cindy

[Chorus]
Cindy Sawfoot is a fucking cunt!
She' a fucking cunt!
She's a fucking cunt!
Cindy Sawfoot is a fucking cunt!
She's a fucking cunt
Yes, she's a fucking cunt

We see **Becky Biro** *taking to Reddit. She is posting several horrible comments about* **Cindy** *and her character.*

Cindy Sawfoot is a fucking cunt!
She's a fucking cunt!
She's a fucking cunt!
Cindy Sawfoot is a fucking cunt!
And I'm gonna shoot her down
Yes, I'm gonna take her down

We see **Becky** *post an old photo of* **Cindy Sawfoot** *on Reddit. She looks busted. She is wearing a t-shirt which says a slur of some kind – which is blurred out to our audience.*

Cindy Sawfoot – she's a fucking cunt!
She's a fucking cunt!
She's a fucking cunt!
Cindy Sawfoot is a fucking cunt!
And I'm gonna prove her wrong
Yes I'm gonna prove her wrong

An absurdist world. It is as if **Becky Biro** *is hosting a talk show and the theatre is her studio audience. Perhaps there's a jingle, a title sequence that plays. There could be video design to punctuate the comedy throughout the scene.*

Becky   Good evening
And welcome back to the sorry state that is my life
In this week's presentation we are going to be exploring the various ways in which I can amass an astronomical social media following in next to no time
We will be weighing up the pros and ignoring the cons of any activities I may take
Or engage in
To achieve the desired results
And lastly we will be comparing each method
Using sophisticated state-of-the-art data analysis
Which consists of counting additional followers
To see which method is indeed the most successful when it comes to building a following as a gender-bending entrepreneur

Option one
The traditional influencer

Pictures pictures pictures
This is all about the pictures you post and the lies they tell about your sad lonely experience
Whether you're on holiday or have abs for days
This is all about targeting those who follow a specific basic hashtag
Like
HashtagTravelgoals
Or
HashtagInstagay
For the travel contingent
Which can gain a surprising amount of followers
I portrayed hashtagqueenonthego
A green screen was required for this
And using basic Zoom backgrounds

I was able to show the world the glamourous jet-setting
lifestyle I lead
From the California
To flying on my private jet
To visiting the Egyptian pyramids
This is all about drawing those fuckers in with your
HashtagLuxuryLifestyle

Perhaps an easier pull for my target audience
My next influencer priority was showing the world that
Becky Biro is a hot commoditiy
In and out of drag
Multiple free trials of Adobe Photoshop using as many fake
email addresses as you possibly can was required for this to
ensure that I was able to take part in the rapidly growing
thirsty phenomenon that is
HashtagTransformationTuesday
For this I simply have to post increasingly thirsty
Bulky
Photoshopped for full effect
Pictures of my body next to a snatched sickening drag
look
These will garner a lot of likes under the guise of your
incredible mind-blowing transformation
But the fact of the matter is
They like these pictures because they wanna come all over
the pumped sweaty naughty chest

The overall result?
Eight hundred and fifty-six followers

Option Two
It's all in the following

Now this one is fairly simple and won't take up much of our
time
This is simply about following as many people as you can
Usually
You don't ever
EVER

Want your following count to be higher than your follower
count
That makes you look desperate
Needy
Like a piece of shit smeared across floor
But Becky Biro ain't no average gal
She's the smartest cookie in that jar
So I followed as many people as my thumbs could possibly
take
Thousands
Tens of thousands
Waited for bitches to follow me back
And then
In the cold dark dead of night
I unfollowed every single one of them bitches
And waited to see how many new followers stuck

I know what you're thinking
You know these people
You look down on these people
But who's laughing when in two years' time they are getting
the job
The validation instead of you because they have the biggest
currency of all
An audience

The result?
One thousand and eighty-one followers

Naughty

Option Three
Manipulate the fandom

Now this one is quite specific to me and my
Well
It's just specific for where I'm at
Fans of cult TV series are
Obsessed
Passionate folk

Enjoying a series can become a hobby in itself
And fans of a certain TV show which I may or may not have
discussed with you already are always on the lookout for
spoilers
Whether that be results of an airing series
Or cast spoilers for who has got a place on an upcoming
season . . .

So in order to gain followers
Go to Reddit
Specifically sub-Reddits of the reality show in question
And post several different upcoming cast spoilers from
several accounts
Differing every time
With one consistent contestant
Becky Biro
Before you know it everyone is talking about it every single
sub-Reddit of the show
And the fandom file in
They want to see who's next

End result
Sixty-three followers

Option four
Fuck it I'll just buy them

If you're pissed off and expecting more followers for all the
hard shitty work you've put in so far
It's time to take things up a notch
Head to your bank account
Empty it
Fuck rent
Fuck food
Fuck everything you need to be alive
You need this more
Take your coins
Take someone else's credit card
Take their coins
And go to the dark web 'cause guess what bitch?

You're gonna buy those followers
And not only that
You can't just buy bots to follow you with no one liking your
posts
That's obvious
You see dumb reality bitches doing that all the time
No
You need to buy the likes
Buy the validation
Buy the validation you deserve
And drink it
Drink it all in
All these bots know who you are
And everyone else thinks you're somebody
Somebody worth following

End result?
Fifty-six thousand followers
Jackpot

Option five
Not safe for work

By this point if you're still not happy you might have started
an OnlyFans
But if you're riddled with internalised sex-positivity shame
like me
There are other smart ways to explore this venture
Something that isn't so open
Something that gets out by accident
Nothing draws the general populous in like the scent of a
scandal

Take a super sexy picture of your most revealing body part
In my case
My overgrown throbbing seeping
Arsehole
Make it look natural
Like you're sending it to that special someone for their eyes
only

Go back to Reddit
Log into that fake account
Trawl through the back end sub-Reddits that follow the show
There is always a NSFW channel
Log in
You have naughty naughty pics of Cindy Sawfoot's bestie
Look at that gaping hole
Isn't it just perfect
So ripe
Glistening in the moonlight
Give them a follow
Here's their at

Result?
Minus five followers
But a few extra likes on those Transformation Tuesdays

The Likes

I want to log off, but something makes me stay
It's the Likes
TikTok and Insta, Twitter and Facebook too
I like Likes
Sometimes it's tough
Some people over share, models in underwear,
Always on holiday,
For the Likes

When I was little, it felt like no one cared,
Unlike Likes
Starved of attention, gay and with low self-esteem,
Give me Likes
I know it's bad
But I can't let it go
I let my mind get boned
Daily by Zuckerberg
But c'mon memes are fun
And nothing validates me
Like your like which masturbates me
Nothing fills the void quite like the Likes

Throughout this number we see **Becky** *scrolling through her social media feed, at various posts which have garnered lots of likes. At the end of the song she stumbles on* **David Peckham**'*s post about their transphobic attack. It has gone viral. It is full of likes and sympathetic comments. The penny drops.*

I've always spent a lot of time on forums
Ever since I was a kid
Growing up as a little pansexual child
Not knowing who I was or finding the words that expressed my gender identity
I was an outsider
Surprise
Or at least I felt like one
And the thing about forums is that they're faceless
You can be whoever you want to be
And somewhere
No matter who you are
Somewhere roaming the dark corners of the internet
Are your people

Growing up my people were pop fanatics
I was obsessed
I wanted to know everything there was to know about my idols
About that life
And I knew my shit
In real life I was a loser but online I was the queen of knowledge when it came to the queen of pop
I knew everything there was to know about Madonna
She was fired from dunkin donuts
She has a fear of thunder
Brontophobia
Gwynneth Paltrow was her maid of honour in two thousand
Like seriously
Come at me
I had the tea and I was adored

In my adult life this love of forums developed into a love of
Reddit
And I think it's because in life
We rightfully have to be so careful about what we say as we
become more awake to societal issues
Thank fuck
I mean that's literally what I preach
But inside there's this other voice in me this
Thing
That just wants to say really
Really bad shit
To experience life with no consequences
And I'm not horrible I just
It's nice to have somewhere to say what I want without fear
of my face
My name being attached to it

I know the type of people who use forums
The core characteristics are true no matter your political or
hate-harbouring beliefs

I know where to go

There are certain corners where a huge contingent of
gender critical arseholes gather
An audience who will despise
Literally refute my existence
Kris's existence
Somewhere they're just huddled together
Spreading their venom
Validating one another along the way

As I'm doing it I obviously, gutturally know that I'm wrong
Kris is lying next to me and I can see his scar
It's like it's glowing at me
Pulsing
I'm thinking about what he'd say
How he'd feel and I
It's not like the abuse will be fake
Hell I've received homophobic

Transphobic
Racist comments my whole life
It's not like it won't be real
It's not like these people who are going to attack don't hold
these views
I'm not creating fake accounts
It's real it's honest I'm just
Steering them in the right direction
I'm turning their canons onto me whilst I'm in the spotlight
Ready for the world to see

It's about time I took these
Experiences I've lived my whole life and turn them into
something positive
Kris isn't the only one who's experienced shit for fuck sake
Look at him now
All the clicks
I've experienced shit too
And I wanna turn that shit into something that positively
Tangibly contributes to my life
My prospects
Because I deserve it
I'm just as talented as any other drag artist and I have
worked for years
I'm sick of being ashamed for wanting recognition
I'm sick of doing things to to make up for it because I think
I'm repulsive for for
Having dreams
For wanting to be loved
For wanting money to to live comfortably
To live gloriously
I deserve the recognition
I deserve to be adored
I don't want my life to be the tragedy of someone who didn't
quite make it
I deserve to rule the world

I sign up
I use the same username as my Reddit one

Cicconne0405
Queen
My birthday
Why not?
No one knows who I am anyway
I'm telling them about this non-binary drag artist
Becky Biro
She bills herself as family friendly
She performs at kids' parties
She fills the kids with trash ideas about a patriarchy
That gender is a construct
That it isn't a binary
She's brainwashing the kids
We must come together to protect our children
She's doing a live
Cheese is lovely
Stupid bitch
Next week
We should tell her about herself
Scare her off of the internet
Indefinitely

It's for the greater good
The good of our children
We must do it for our children

Will You Follow Me *Reprise – To be played / sung in between Acts
Two and Three.*

Fuck you Becky Biro
You're a bitch and a bad person
With each new thing that comes to light
Your reputation worsens
You're a whore
You are a nasty piece of shit
Smeared on the floor

I hate you Becky Biro
You're no better than the bigots
You used us up and spat us out
An evil cow, malicious
Hope you die
Yeah fuck you bitch I hope you cry
And die die die

Go unfollow Becky B
Do not follow Becky B
If you follow Becky B
Then you are as bad as she
Are as bad as she

Three

The UK Drag Council's Town Hall on the subject of Becky Biro and what's to be done with her

A Zoom meeting appears. All the characters in this scene are in video design apart from **Becky** *and those otherwise stated.* **Jackie Beaver** *and* **Voica Reesin** *are present at all times and all other characters are brought in and out as stated in the scene.*

Jackie   Now I'm very excited for everyone who can join us for this evening's open discussion Brought to you by Morgan Stanley
Lloyds Bank
Costa Coffee The NHS
Sketchers
Slim Chickens Greggs
Clifford Chance
Heinz Beans
Dominoes Pizza Ireland's Twitter account
The sex shop on the A1 just off the northbound carriageway between Doncaster and Pontefract
Zara

St Margaret's Church and Community Choir
And Tesco
Because every little helps

Right
Now I believe that
Um
Given the
Event
Of which the true nature has been made so public over the
last few months
And given the Queen-in-question's role in our community
We feel that now is an appropriate time to
Uh
Go ahead and get some stuff off of our chests
Because a lot has been said
Online
And it's about time we sit down and
Have the conversations that need to be had
And I'm very excited for us all to be together to come to a
resolution
Voica

Voica   Yes hello everyone
For those of you who don't know me I'm Voica Reesin and
Jackie has very kindly asked me to be your official mediator
for this evening
My role will be to mediate the conversation and keep us on
track to ensure that we are working towards a resolution
I know it's a very emotional affair but I will be working to
keep the emotion out and have us working towards practical
steps of action

Jackie   I do want to go over some ground rules initially
Firstly I want to honour the courage of all the speakers
tonight
I know that at events such as this in the past that things have
got quite
Heated

And people have been forcibly removed
But I do want to state that as long as we have reasonable behaviour
No one will be excluded from this meeting
But as your elected chairman
If you disrupt this meeting I do maintain the right to remove you

Okay so firstly
Let's bring in –

A blank screen entitled **'Julie's iPad'** *appears on the screen.*

Julie's iPad   Hello?
Oh 'iya love
I'm just in a meeting can I call ya back later?

Voica   Can someone remove Julie's iPad please?

Julie's iPad   I said I'm just in a meeting can I call you back later?
Yes I'm alright thanks love

I was saying I'm just in a meeting

Voica   Anyone?

Julie's iPad   Yes
Alright t'ra love

I said t'ra lo –

Julie's iPad *is removed from the meeting.*

Jackie   Okay
Sorry about that
Please can we bring in Becky Biro

Becky *is brought into the meeting; she is live on stage whilst the rest of the characters are framed in the Zoom meeting. An* **Albert Brewerton** *is now visible on the Zoom meeting having been brought on at the same time.*

Jackie   Becky are you with us?

Becky

Jackie   Becky you're on mute

Becky   Yes I'm here

Thanks so much for giving me the time and space –

Albert   She's kicked her out

Becky   Um

Time and space to be held accountable for my actions –

Albert   She's kicked her out

Voica   I'm sorry who are you?

Albert   Julie's iPad
She's kicked out Julie's iPad

Jackie   As your elected chair
I have the authority to –

Albert   No you don't because I'm vice-chair

Jackie   What are you talking about?

Albert   We're trying to have a Teams meeting you fool
We can't if you (Unintelligible hissing.)

Voica   Excuse me?

Jackie   Does anybody know who this cis man is?

Albert   I take charge
Read the standing orders
READ THEM AND UNDERSTAND THEM

You have no authority here Jackie Beaver
No authority at all

Albert *is removed from the meeting.*

Jackie   ANYBODY ELSE?

Right

Voica   Let's continue

Jackie   Becky Biro
We are gathered here today to review the impact your
actions have had on the community you serve
On the individuals within it
And to decide the best course of action to take going
forwards

Before we bring in the various speakers I want to say that
you will have the opportunity to speak when we permit you
to do so
You are not to interrupt or disrespect the speakers
Do you understand?

Becky   Yes
I do

Jackie   If you have anything you would like to say to the
council before we begin now is your time to do so
The floor is yours

Becky   Okay so
Firstly
I want to say that I'm really sorry if my actions hurt anyone's
feelings

Before Drag Factor I was really poor and I often missed out
on gigs because of my selfless activism on social media
It got to the point where I was finding it really hard to pay
for day to day things like food and cannabis
This had a severe impact on my mental health and clouded
my judgement
And it is then that I did what I did

I understand that it is not okay to fake or engineer a hate
crime for my own financial gain but I do have to say that I
am really not a bad person
I understand the gravity of what I did but I don't think that
people should be sending me abuse
I've lost my job
Haven't I suffered enough?

Sometimes in life we make mistakes
I am only human after all

Thank you for listening to my apology
It is really hard living with what I have done
I am really tired and sad

Voica   O-kay

Jackie   Our first speaker today is
Aveek Tim
Aveek is here to bring charges including a loss of income and
emotional turmoil
Voica can we bring her in please

Aveek Tim *is brought visibly into the meeting. When she is brought
in she appears as an animated cat.*

Voica   Hello
Aveek are you present?

Aveek   Yes I'm here

Jackie   Aveek I think you've got a filter on

Aveek   Sorry?

Voica   You've got a filter on

Aveek   Have I?
Sorry I've turned off self-view

Jackie   Can you turn it off?

Aveek   Sorry so sorry

Jackie   That's okay

Aveek   Am I good now?

Jackie   You're still a cat Aveek

Aveek   I don't know how to turn it off
It's me I promise
I'm not lying
I'm not actually a
Cat

Voica   I'm conscious of time

Aveek   I'm happy to carry on if you are
I can just
Say what I've gotta say

Voica   Jackie?

Jackie   Go ahead Aveek

Aveek   Okay
So
I want to start by thanking the UK Drag Council for having me
And for giving me this platform to
To speak my truth

This has been a really hard time for me
I was a huge fan of Becky Biro
I've obviously worked with her a lot and because of that I've had a really hard time getting work myself
My shows have been under her umbrella and people think that I was somehow in
On what she did
So my career has really suffered as a direct result of her actions

Also as someone who experiences violent hate crimes online
Regularly
I can tell you that it isn't something to trivialise
I lose sleep over the comments I receive
Telling me that I'm a no good
That I'm a filthy good for nothing faggot

Becky *laughs. She covers it up.*

Aveek   That I should be killed for merely existing
That I should go ahead and get hit by a car
Or be murdered
Taken out and buried in the garden

Becky *laughs again.*

Voica   I'm sorry Aveek
Becky is something funny?

Becky   No no
Sorry I just had something up my
Nose
I
Sorry please continue

Aveek   I think Becky's actions
Which have been made so public
Have really emboldened people who say that homophobic
Transphobic and racist abuse no longer exists
That if we take offence it's our fault
That we're just a bunch of pussies

Becky *bursts into laughter.*

Becky   I'm sorry
I'm so sorry

Aveek   Is something funny?

Becky   I'm sorry

Aveek   You're disgusting

Voica   This isn't going anywhere

Jackie   Becky you clearly aren't processing the severity of
the situation
I would have thought that months with no work
No income and no place in the community might have made
you realise the affect your actions have had on people
And that maybe today we could work together
For you
To find a place for you in the community
For you to atone for what you did
To start the process of forgiveness
We can just pull the plug on this right now?

Becky   No
Please

I'm sorry I'm nervous and it's just her filter
I swear
Don't
Don't end this

Voica   Do you promise to listen
To give space to the remaining speakers this evening?

Becky   Yes
I promise

Jackie   Next to speak we have Cindy Sawfoot
A shining example of an exceptional entertainer who
wholesomely gives back to the community she serves
And who we are very proud to announce as our official
ambassador for Action of Progress and Change
Cindy I'm sure I speak on behalf of everyone at the council
in saying thank you for driving our cause forward

Everyone claps apart from **Becky**.

Becky   Are you fucking –

Jackie   Mute her

Becky *is muted.*

Jackie   Due to ongoing tour commitments Cindy cannot be
with us tonight
She's recorded the following message

A video of **Cindy** *appears. She is framed perfectly next to placed
bottles of Rio with an open can she is drinking from with a straw.*

Cindy   Hello everyone
It's ya girl Cindy Sawfoot here
I'm gutted that I can't be with you on what is a night that
represents a great opportunity for our community to be the
change we want to see in this world

Cindy *takes a contrived sip of Rio.*

Becky Biro has hurt the community with her despicable
Selfish actions

I know I sit here in a privileged position as someone who is
incredibly successful
With a huge platform
And that other people have been more negatively affected by
her actions
But Becky Biro tried to ruin my life on several occasions
I had long suspected Becky was behind the account
Cicconne0405 on an internet forum site known as Reddit
This account forged problematic photos of me
Said that I was difficult to work with
And even called me a cunt
Sorry was I not supposed to
But it was when I saw the posts from Cicconne0405 on
ParentsWeb that I had the confirmation that it was truly her
And that was why I felt the need to speak out

She takes another sip of Rio.

There are those present in the meeting tonight that have lost
money because of her actions
According to my sources at the UK Drag Council-tm
This is believed to be in the region on twenty-five thousand
pounds
I demand that Becky repays this debt to UK Drag Council
who will then use this money to give back to the drag
community and raise awareness of LGBTQ+ hate crimes
A percentage will also go to charity

She takes another sip of Rio.

This is my demand
This is what I demand for Becky to continue working
People like her must be held accountable for their actions if
we are to move forwards as one
We deserve reparations
The community deserves reparations

She takes another sip of Rio.

Thank you all for being so generous with your time
Be sure to follow the UK Drag Council to support all the
good they do for our community

*She waves goodbye, holding the Rio can aloft. The message ends and
we snap back into the Zoom meeting.*

Voica   So that is an example of tangible action
Something solid that begins to make amends for the damage
you've caused

Becky   I can't afford that

Voica   It's very generous that Cindy wants to donate the
money to such a good cause

Becky   I can't afford it

Voica   We would propose that this is some kind of payment
plan to us and a charity over a number of years
It's not about repaying the exact amount but the point is you
are paying back into organisations which will work against
the types of crime you fraudulently exploited for your own
monetary gain

Becky   I said I can't afford that
I can't do that

Jackie   Well you need to pay something

Okay our next speaker is David Peckham who we all know
used to have a close
Intimate friendship with Becky prior to all of this
Can we bring in David please?

David Peckham *is brought into the Zoom meeting.*

Jackie   David can you hear us?

David   I can hear you perfectly

Jackie   Thank you so much for joining us this evening

David   Thank you for having me

Jackie   If you wouldn't mind
Could you speak about the impact of Becky's actions on your
career
And what you think she can do to make this right?

David   Of course
So –

Becky   Kris
C'mon

Voica   Becky

Becky   It's me
I said I'm sorry

Voica   Becky you're gonna need to be quiet and let David
speak
Immediately

David   We've seen the girls and a
Cat
Talk about money so far
Which is ironic in some ways
Given they have the lion share of it in this industry
And don't get me wrong I've lost earnings
What little I had of them yeah that fucking
Dried up quickly
But what I don't think you understand is the
Impact
The the the consequences of what you've done

I want to start with
Just
A trigger warning
Violence to an LGBT+ person

Last year
When I was attacked for being who I am
Becky nursed me when I got home

When they attacked me they hit me from behind
They called me a freak
A paedophile
It was the stone
They hit me with a stone just grabbed it from someone's
garden
It fractured my skull
It took me
Months
Just to learn how to walk again

It was the darkest time of my life and it was Becky who saw
me through that

Becky   Kris
Please
I'm sorry

David   So the idea that she would
Engineer
This kind of abuse for herself
Just to get on a shit reality show
For people to know who she is
It makes me sick to my stomach

The same girl that held my hand as I lay /there

Becky   Kris
I'm sorry

David   Right now there is a real threat to the human rights
of trans people
The mob which you saw pile on Becky is real

These people thought that I made it up
The attack
They thought that I lied
That I paid someone to do it to me to further my career
They'll think that of others now
When they go through this shit

That's the damage you've done
That's the damage you've done Becky

There is no forgiveness
For me
There can be no forgiveness

Becky   I did it for you
Your queen in shining stillettos
I was gonna get us a flat
It was all for –

Voica   David Peckham
What do you want to see happen now
What are the first steps Becky can take to
Pay
For what she's done

Becky   I said I'm sorry
Please

David   I'm not necessarily her biggest fan but Cindy's right

Becky   Really?
You're on that train now?

David   Becky needs to pay charities to
She needs a payment plan
Look at what she can afford a month and set up a plan
Indefinitely

Jackie   Becky is this something you can agree to?

Becky   I don't work
No one will book me
How can I pay if you won't let me work?

David   She needs to repurpose her social media so it's not
performative anymore
Take her face off it
She needs to dedicate her platform to good causes
She needs to raise awareness

Becky   Kris stop it
I'm not deleting shit

Voica   He's not asking you to delete –

David   I am
She hasn't learnt
She hasn't
She doesn't care
She isn't taking any accountability for what she's done

I want her to disappear
I want her to disappear for a long time to to to
Think about what she's done

I want her gone

Jackie   You think she should be deplatformed?

Becky   This is insane
Fuckoff
All of you can fuckoff

David   Yes

Voica   All in favour of this notion please say aye

Becky   What?
You don't have the right
The authority

David   Aye

Jackie   Aye

Voica   Aye

Becky   You can't vote you're the mediator
You can't vote

Aveek   Aye

Becky   I won't do it
You can't make me

Don't Delete Me

They all want to dispose of me
Make a queen like me feel small
But just like Jesy Nelson
I'll rise above it all

Fine, I'm not proud
Of the things you say
I did which do sound bad
But I am more
Than one mistake
So I'm sorry that you're mad

But unless you are perfect
And never done wrong
Don't delete me
We each have a moment
Where it's us all along
Don't delete me
There are so many monsters who deeply deserve
To be cancelled before little me
Kevin Spacey, Sherry Pie, delete them,
Just don't delete me

I've always had my problems
Struggles with my mental health
My Pen-pals give me purpose
Take them and I will kill myself

You laugh but the trolls
Are in my DMs
Telling me to kill myself too
And so if I die
There's blood on your hands
Yes that shit will all be on you

So unless you are perfect
And never done wrong
Don't delete me
We each have a moment

Where it's us all along
Don't delete me
How come Cindy gets given full amnesty
Did y'all forget I too was on TV
I was made to be famous
You cannot, cannot delete me

You loved me before
But now that's no more
I've said sorry and I've even cried
What more do you want?
Make a martyr of me?
Then fine, I will be crucified
Crucified
You can't delete me
Like, Jesus Christ
You can't delete me

You have taken this mob justice people's court zoom
meeting thing a little bit too far
You can ask me to leave
But you better believe
That you cannot delete
Becky B
A legend, an icon, a motherfucking star

Jackie   Becky?

Becky Biro
Are you with us?

Becky   Yes

Jackie   The people have spoken
You need to take some time away to think about what you've
done
You need to listen and learn
You are to delete yourself
Entirely

Do you understand?

Becky   But what am I supposed to do now?

Jackie   Exist somewhere
Invisibly

Are there any final things you would like to say?

Becky?

Becky   I'm sorry
I'm so sorry

NO –

Blackout.

End.